Biblical answers to bothersome Questions

Bob Jones III

BOB JONES UNIVERSITY PRESS

Biblical Answers to Bothersome Questions

by Bob Jones III

©1981 Bob Jones University Press
Greenville, South Carolina 29614
ISBN 0-89084-150-0

Printed in the United States of America

20 19 18 17 16 15 14 13 12 11 10 9 8 7

Contents

Question 1

Is the Bible reliable?

Many people say that the Bible is not reliable. The Lord Jesus Christ, in Matthew 5:18, says, "Till heaven and earth pass, one jot or one tittle shall in no wise pass from the law, till all be fulfilled."

Jesus Christ was a truthful man. Indeed, He was the God-man and could not lie; and He says that the hills would sooner be leveled with the plains, and the stars would sooner fall from their sockets than the smallest part of His Word should fail in its fulfillment. The *jot* is the smallest letter in the Hebrew alphabet. The *tittle* is the small, almost imperceptible change from letter to letter that alters the meaning of those letters. It is the difference in rounding a corner as opposed to having a square corner. The Lord Jesus was saying, "My Word is so precise and so true that even the most substantial things on earth will sooner disappear than that any part of My Word shall fail to be fulfilled." These are strong words, and the skeptics had better stand up and take notice.

John Wesley, the great English preacher, said that it was his feeling that the Bible could have come from only three possible sources: good men or angels, bad men or devils, or God Himself. Good men and angels, he said, would not and could not write a good book that would at the same time tell lies; and if the Bible is not the authoritative, God-given Word to man from heaven, it is telling a lie because that is what it claims to be. Bad men or devils would not have produced this book, he said, because it commands all to obey, condemns sinners to hell, and is intolerant of sin. Certainly bad men could not have written the Book, so that leaves only God Himself as its Source.

People who say that the Bible is not God's Word must concede at least three things. In the first place, they must say that it is not a good book. If this book is a good book, it is good only because it is divine and trustworthy. The Bible is in contrast to the uncertainty of all ordinary books. If it is not without error, this book must be classified with every other book in the world. If it is not *all* true, what part of it is true and what part is false? Are you willing to make that judgment? Is it ninety percent true and ten percent false? Is it ten percent true and ninety percent false? If you are not willing to take all of the Bible as His Word, you must decide which part is true and which is false. That makes you the judge of the book which claims to judge you. This book then becomes subordinated to the standard against which its truth is measured. If the Bible is what it claims to be, it must be all true and therefore all trustworthy.

In the second place, those who say that this book is not the Word of God must concede that Jesus Christ is either a liar, a fraud, or a bigot, for Jesus Christ treated the Law, the Prophets, and the Psalms as a solid structure of historical fact and supernatural process. Throughout His ministry, He quoted Scripture. In Luke 4:18, He preached in the synagogue at Nazareth. Opening the Scriptures to Isaiah 61, He read the Messianic promise of His first advent. He stopped reading, closed the book, and told His audience that the Scripture was fulfilled in Himself.

In Luke 24, the Lord Jesus is pictured walking down the road with two of His disciples who were discouraged, thinking that His body had been stolen. They were reluctant to believe all of the rumors of His bodily resurrection from the grave. When the Lord joined them, it was as a stranger. Scripture says that "their eyes were holden that they should not know him" (verse 16). He listened to their conversation for a few moments; then He began at "Moses and all the prophets" and preached unto them "in all the scriptures the things concerning himself." In other words, the Lord Jesus started with Genesis and continued through the Old Testament Scriptures that spoke of Him. He *believed* in the reliability of the Scriptures. In the twelfth chapter of Matthew, He spoke about the fact that as Jonah was three days and three nights in the belly of the fish, so

must He—the Son of Man—be three days and
three nights in the belly of the earth. His frame
of reference was to the time between His
crucifixion and His bodily resurrection from the
grave. He took the most disputed and scorned of
all passages by the "liberals" today—the passage which deals with Jonah's being literally
swallowed into the belly of the fish—and says,
"This is a literal truth. And as this truth is
literal, so I am telling you literally that I am
going to spend the same amount of time in the
heart of the earth." Dear friends, the Bible is
indeed an anvil against which all the hammers
of the skeptics are worn out.

In the third place, to deny that the Bible is
God's authoritative Word is to concede that it is
not only inaccurate, but also a calculated lie. The
Bible says that it is God-breathed. According to
II Peter 1:21, "Holy men of God spake as they
were moved by the Holy Ghost." According to
II Timothy 3:16, "All scripture is given by
inspiration of God." The word *inspiration* means
"God-breathed." It conveys, in the strongest
possible terms, the meaning that the Bible is of
divine origin and authority. The divine superin-
tendence over the sacred writers of the Bible
guarantees that their writings are trustworthy,
free of error in fact and in doctrine. The writers
of Scripture realized that they were not giving
their own opinions. Seven times in chapters two
and three of Revelation, John says, "He that
hath an ear, let him hear *what the Spirit* saith
unto the churches" [emphasis mine]. John knew
that he was not giving his own thoughts. Again,
in II Peter 1:21, Peter says that "the prophecy

came not in old time by the will of man: but holy men of God spake as they were moved [borne along] by the Holy Ghost." The word *moved* or *borne along* is the same word which Paul uses in Acts 27 when he speaks of his ship's being in a storm and being borne along by the power of the storm. In Galatians 1:11, 12, Paul says, "I certify you, brethren [that is the same as saying, "I swear to you"], that the gospel which was preached of me is not after man. For I neither received it of man, neither was I taught it, but by the revelation of Jesus Christ." The Lord Jesus Christ, not the writers, is responsible for the trustworthiness of the Scripture. The prophets did not originate the Scripture; they were merely spokesmen of Scripture.

When we say that the Bible is without error, we are referring to the original manuscripts—the Greek, Hebrew, and Aramaic manuscripts—not the various translations of the Bible. Copyists make errors. But God-fearing scholars have brought translations to a high state of accuracy, so that the form in which we have the Bible today is substantially identical with the original manuscripts.

You ask, "Which translation of the Bible should I use?" My answer is that you should use the one that is closest to the original languages. That rules out all paraphrases, such as *Good News For Modern Man, The Living Bible,* or whatever paraphrase you may think is good. Paraphrasing Scripture is simply man's putting into his own words what he *thinks* the Scripture says. If you have only a paraphrase of the Bible, you do not have the Bible. You have merely a commentary on the Scriptures. You do not have the true words of Scripture; you have what man *thinks* it says.

A great man has said that potentates have proclaimed their edicts, tyrants have lighted up their fires, and mercenary legions have shed rivers of human blood in order to destroy the Bible and its beliefs. In spite of them all, however, this book lives on. The more men have tried to eradicate the Bible, the more deeply they have planted the roots. The more they have tried to blot out the Name of Christ, the more legible and glorious it has become. Yes, the Lord has said, "Heaven and earth may pass away, but my words shall not pass away."

Christian friend, dust off the covers of your Bible. Open it, and let its divine, inerrant, authoritative, verbally inspired, forever-settled-in-heaven Word enter your heart and become the foundation of all your practice and the life-giving water to your dry and thirsty soul.

Question 2

Who is Jesus?

I call your attention to a newspaper article which appeared some time ago in a major newspaper. An article of this type is so absurd, so blatant and ridiculous that it hardly deserves serious attention on the part of God's people. But it provides a launching pad for the question, Who is Jesus? The author of this article, the head of the Bible department at a state university, was addressing a group of atheists who had invited him to discuss with them how they could cope with zealous Christian evangelists on the streets who tried to convert them to the knowledge of the Lord Jesus Christ. The speaker said to the atheists, "Jesus never really claimed to be God or to be related to Him." He described Christianity as having gone astray and said that "Paul, Matthew, Mark, Luke, and John bear

much of the blame." He said further that
"Christianity started as an ethical movement
devoted to service" and that Christ was put to
death for a mistake that He made. I want to
challenge this man's statements as we look at
the Word of God and seek to answer the question,
Who is Jesus?

First of all, the speaker said that Jesus never
claimed to be God. That Jesus Christ is God
come in human flesh is the proposition upon
which Christianity stands. Over and over the
Lord asserted His deity. In John 14:6-9 "Jesus
saith unto him [Thomas], I am the way, the
truth, and the life: no man cometh unto the
Father, but by me. If ye had known me, ye
should have known my Father also: and from
henceforth ye know him, and have seen him.
Philip saith unto him, Lord, shew us the Father,
and it sufficeth us. Jesus saith unto him, Have
I been so long time with you, and yet hast thou
not known me, Philip? he that hath seen me hath
seen the Father." In John 8:56-59, the Lord said
to the people who did not believe Him, "Your
father Abraham rejoiced to see my day: and he
saw it, and was glad. Then said the Jews unto
him, Thou art not yet fifty years old, and hast
thou seen Abraham? Jesus said unto them,
Verily, verily, I say unto you, Before Abraham
was, I am. Then took they up stones to cast at
him." They understood! He said, "I am the great
I Am," which is the word reserved for Jehovah,
the eternal God of Glory. He claimed that title for
Himself, and those who rejected His deity tried
to kill Him for making that claim.

The Lord Jesus, during His earthly ministry,

received the worship of men, and no one except God has the right to be worshipped by man. If Jesus Christ is not God, He was a fraud; He was insane; He was the most preposterous individual who ever lived on the face of the earth. But the religion which Jesus Christ founded is the purest religion that is known to man; and those who believe in Him become pure. Their sins are forgiven, and they walk in the righteousness of the Lord Jesus and in newness of life. No fraud could produce that kind of religion; nor could believing in a fraud produce that kind of person.

Next, the speaker said that Christianity has gone astray and that "Paul, Matthew, Mark, Luke, and John" are responsible for it. The Lord Jesus was not invented by the evangelists to whom this man has referred. Only Jesus could "invent" a Jesus. That these evangelists could have produced a Jesus strains credulity. Matthew, Mark, Luke, John, and Paul merely speak to us of the only sinless One Who ever lived. The Lord Jesus said, "I am the light of the world" (John 8:12). Consider the audacity of that claim! The Lord was speaking to some harlots, Pharisees, false religious leaders, tax collectors, and fishermen. He said, "I am the light of the world." Neither Socrates, Plato, nor Moses ever made that claim. Only the God of heaven could make such a claim truthfully.

The Apostle Peter walked with the Lord, wrote about the Lord, witnessed of the Lord, and gave his life for the testimony of the resurrection of Jesus Christ; and he said in his second epistle, "We have not followed cunningly devised fables, when we made known unto you the power and coming of our Lord Jesus Christ" (1:16). Peter also declared that "no prophecy of the scripture is of any private interpretation." That is, "Nobody invented what we said. We did not make it up. We know the One of Whom we speak. We have walked with Him and lived with Him. We have seen Him and have heard His claims; and He *is* the One He claims to be. He is God come in human flesh."

The author from whose article we have quoted said further that Christianity has been perverted into a movement of salvation rather than of service. The Gospels present the Lord Jesus without sin, and nowhere else in literature or history do we find such a man. No, my dear friend, He Who is the sinless Son of God came to bear your sin and mine in His own body on the Cross. He said, "I did not come to call the righteous, but sinners to repentance." The Lord Jesus is the best friend any sinner ever had; yet some of you are running from Him. Perhaps someone handed you a gospel tract one day and told you that you needed the Lord Jesus to save you from your sin. But you have rebelled at the thought of being a sinner and having to depend upon the righteousness of Jesus Christ. Sinner, He is the best friend you will ever have. He is the friend of sinners, and He came to die for you. He is salvation, for "there is none other name under heaven given among men, whereby we must be saved" (Acts 4:12). You need Him. Won't you trust Him today—trust the God of Glory as your Saviour and be saved from your sin?

Question 3

What is Christianity?

What a difference it would make in America if everyone who called himself a Christian were indeed a Christian. According to Acts 11:26, "the disciples were called Christians first in Antioch." No doubt the term, as it was initially used, was a term of derision. But the disciples in Antioch deserved the appellation "Christian." When a man is deservedly referred to as a Christian, it is because he leaves no doubt about Who his master is.

Suppose you were on trial for being a Christian. Would there be enough evidence to convict you? A Gallup poll predicted that 1976 would be considered the year of the evangelical. According to this poll, one-half of all Protestants and one-third of all Americans say they are born again. What they *say*, however, has no resemblance to what they *are*. If fifty percent of all Protestants really knew Jesus Christ, America would not be the heathen nation that it is. It takes more than a label to be a Christian; it takes a life—a life that begins in Jesus Christ and a life that continues in Jesus Christ. It is not enough to say that a number of years ago you had some kind of experience that made you a Christian. If you have been made a Christian through faith in the shed blood of the Lord Jesus Christ, you will continue in Christ.

An evangelist held a meeting in a certain church. After one of the services an irate woman approached him and said, "I do not like your kind of preaching. I do not like to hear about the blood of Jesus Christ. Why don't you talk about the good works of people? Why don't you discuss living a good moral life or walking in the footsteps of Jesus? I try to do that every day of my life." The evangelist answered, "If you really walked in the footsteps of Jesus, you would have to start in the first step. According to I Peter 2:22, Jesus Christ 'did no sin.' If you can honestly put your foot in that footprint, you can put your foot in the rest of His footprints." The woman went away angrier than ever, because he had touched her problem.

Perhaps that is your problem. Perhaps you have tried to live as you think a Christian ought to live, but you have not been washed from your sin in the blood of Jesus Christ. If that is the case, you have not been born again, and you are not a Christian. The Christian life starts at Calvary.

John Wesley defined Christianity as "the life

of God in the souls of men." Wherever the life of God is found, it is evidenced by a pure life. I cannot have much faith in a profession of Christianity when the one who professes it does not contribute to that which a Christian should leave in this world. A true Christian will leave behind him the mark of purity. I know people who claim to be Christians; but instead of contributing Christian purity to this world, they contribute to the world's debauched rock culture. They sing rock songs that contain some quasi-religious words that talk about Jesus. They frequent nightclubs and drink booze, and they throw a little crumb to Jesus. There are many nightclub entertainers who call themselves Christians. They perform in Las Vegas or in some local club. They entertain boozers, wife swappers, and debauched and blaspheming people; and then in the middle of their program they sing a few songs about Jesus. They seem to think that the use of a few religious songs will vindicate all the harm they are doing. I receive letters from people who defend these rock idols. They ask, "How could you be against the rock culture? How could you criticize these rock singers?" They extol the rock performers; then they add: "I have watched these singers stand on the platform in the middle of their nightclub acts and sing 'How Great Thou Art' or 'The Battle Hymn of the Republic.' I have seen the tears stream down the faces of these entertainers." My friend, singing religious songs and weeping will not make a person a Christian. A man who has been to the cross and has been saved from his unrighteousness will not continue to honor an unrighteous lifestyle.

There are people who call themselves Christians and are very religious. But they deny that Jesus Christ is the Son of God; and in denying the claims our Lord made about Himself, these so-called Christians make Christ a liar.

Hans Kung, the Catholic author of a new book entitled *On Being A Christian,* expresses doubt that Jesus Christ pre-existed in the Godhead before His human birth. This book has sold 150,000 copies in Germany and now is being printed by Doubleday. Though Kung calls himself a Christian, he doubts many of Christ's miracles and considers the story of the virgin birth "largely legendary." There are countless men who express doubts about the deity of Christ and yet claim to be Christians.

What is a Christian? A Christian is a blood-washed follower of Christ. Being a Christian also involves denying oneself. Our Lord said in Matthew 16:24, "If any man will come after me, let him deny himself, and take up his cross, and follow me." This means that we must deny all our opinions and attitudes and goals that are contrary to Christ.

Taking up our cross daily and following Jesus Christ will limit our circle of friends. We will not keep company with people who scoff at Jesus Christ and His deity; nor will we engage in activities and habits that are at variance with, and in contradiction to, the precious Word of God.

Furthermore, the scope of the things we approve will be limited. There are some people to whom we cannot say, "God bless you." It does not matter how renowned a man may be in the religious world—if he denies the deity of Jesus Christ, it is wrong for us to say to him, "God bless you," for he is a deceiver and an antichrist (II John 10, 11).

There is only one kind of Christian, and that is the Christian who has come to the foot of the cross and said, "God be merciful to me, a sinner"—the Christian who has been transformed by the saving grace of Jesus Christ and who continually walks with Christ. True Christians are narrow. The *Encyclopaedia Britannica* says, "Christianity is the most widely diffused of all religions geographically. It has a membership of one billion people." The Bible says otherwise. The Bible says, "Narrow is the way, which leadeth unto life, and few there be that find it" (Matthew 7:14). Even fewer are those who walk on that road in a manner that will reveal to an observer that they are heaven-bound.

In the Aleutian Islands there is a tribe of Eskimos called Diomedes. Their island— a mountain—is two and a half miles long, one and a half miles wide, and most unattractive. All year they are beset by fierce northern storms and are shrouded in fog. Their population is 120, and they are loyal to their island, their heritage, and their ancient way of life. The government has offered to move the people off the island and house them in a better place, but the offers are spurned. These people are determined to endure the hardships on their island in order to remain free from the mainland way of life.

The world talks of "better things," but the

Christian must resist. He must remain "unmove-able, always abounding in the work of the Lord" (I Corinthians 15:58). I do not merely look forward to my eternal life, my heavenly life, with Jesus Christ; I am enjoying this earthly road, because Jesus Christ walks with me and I with Him. Jesus Christ makes life worth living.

It is time for true Christians to take a stand for Jesus Christ and move out of their liberal, Christ-denying churches. It is time that true Christians shed the shackles of denominational loyalty and put their loyalty with Jesus Christ their Saviour. In your area there are fundamental churches that preach the true gospel of the saving grace of Jesus Christ through faith in His shed blood; churches that lift up this book—the Word of God—and walk in the Word and honor it, and that judge all things according to Scripture instead of man's opinions. A true Christian needs to be in the right kind of church.

For the sake of your souls, the testimony of your Saviour, and your witness to a lost and hell-bound mankind, you need to be in a sound, Christ-honoring church. You need to let your light shine so that men may see your good works and glorify your Father which is in heaven (Matthew 5:16).

Question 4

Can a Christian control his thought life?

How many times have we picked up a newspaper and learned of a great tragedy—some mass killing, bank robbery, or terrible perversion—and thought, "How terrible it is that suddenly a life which apparently was headed in another direction was involved in a crime so terrible!"

This kind of thing does not happen suddenly. That which made the headlines was merely the outcropping of something that had been going on for a long time inside the heart and mind of that individual. My grandfather used to say, "Back of every tragedy of human character there is a process of wicked thinking."

I suppose that more Christians have problems in their thought life than perhaps any other area. Perhaps you are a person who outwardly is quite refined and decent and wholesome. Nobody has any idea of the vulgarities, the obscenities, and the blasphemies that are being hatched and formulated in your mind. Scripture says that as a man "thinketh in his heart, so is he" (Proverbs 23:7). It is not what people think you are, or even what you think you are, that reveals what you are. It is what you think that reveals what you are.

If you would be completely honest with yourself and tell me what you are thinking today, I could tell you where you will be five years from now if God does not get hold of you and turn you around. You do not go anywhere that your thoughts do not precede you. Suppose you walk past a bank on the way to work and you think, "It wouldn't be too hard for somebody to rob that bank. It is not well protected." Every day you walk by that bank you think that same thought. One day it dawns on you, "I could rob that bank." Soon you find yourself formulating a means whereby you might perform the act; and if something does not stop you, you will rob the bank and when apprehended will spend a large part of your life in jail.

You may be a fine church member—fine as far as your friends and your pastor or Sunday school teacher know—but you are thinking indecent thoughts. You may, on the sly, be reading "girlie" magazines and filling your mind with nudity. It will not be long until you find yourself being unfaithful to your wife—committing an act of adultery or fornication. People will say, "What a tragedy! We thought that he was a good family man. We regarded him as a fine Christian." You have fooled people for a time. Nobody knew that you were filling your thoughts with filth that would erupt one day in a horrifying act.

Did you ever watch an icicle form? It is a beautiful sight when the water that forms it is clean and pure and free of sediment. If the water has dirt in it, however, the icicle will be dirty. It will be a brown or muddy gray and far from beautiful. When the icicle is formed of dirty water, the sunshine cannot reflect from it any of the colors of the rainbow.

Your life is like that. If the thoughts that make up your life are clean and pure and decent, your life will be pure. It will be clean and beautiful. But if the thoughts are dirty, sooner or later people will look upon a dirty life.

A person's thinking is influenced basically by what he sees, what he hears, what he reads, and what he does. It is important that you read the right things and that you listen to the right things. You need to be influenced by the right kind of influences, because eventually those influences will produce either good acts or bad acts.

If you are having trouble with your thinking, Christian friend, turn to your Bible. In it is the solution to your problem. The Scripture gives three guiding principles upon which you can base a clean thought life. First of all, you can *corral bad thoughts*. That is, you can put a fence around them. Paul wrote to the Corinthians of "bringing into captivity every thought to the obedience of Christ" (II Corinthians 10:5). Either you will capture your evil thoughts, or they will capture you. Corral them. Do not let them spread any further.

Next, you can *substitute clean thoughts for unclean thoughts.* In Philippians 4:8 Paul says, "Finally, brethren, whatsoever things are true, whatsoever things are honest, whatsoever things are just, whatsoever things are pure, whatsoever things are lovely, whatsoever things are of good report; if there be any virtue, and if there be any praise, think on these things." Get your thoughts off the bad things, and think on good things. According to Scripture, the substitution of good thoughts will purge the wicked thoughts.

Finally, *"Commit thy works* unto the Lord, and thy thoughts shall be established" (Proverbs 16:3). If your works are to make Christ known, to win souls for Him, to live your life for the good of others, or to see the devil's plan for this world defeated, your indulgence in these good works will guarantee that your thoughts will dwell on these subjects. The person who gets into trouble with his thought life is the person who is not committed to doing the will of God, who does not have goals or motivations for the investment of his life in Christian service, who is grudging with the time he gives to the Lord, and who spends his time in selfish pursuits. God's book is the only solution to our problems, and it is forever settled in heaven (Psalm 119:89).

Question 5

What is the gospel?

There are many perversions of the gospel in our land and much misunderstanding about what the gospel really is. If we can help clarify this subject in your thinking by giving you a Scriptural understanding of the gospel, it may make the difference in where you will spend eternity.

Many of you have believed the gospel and have been saved by the gospel. But with all the strange ideas that are spread abroad, you have become confused. I believe that if you have a clear understanding of what the Bible teaches about the gospel, you will employ your life in a proper giving of the gospel to other people.

The Apostle Paul said, "For I am not ashamed of the gospel of Christ: for it is the power of God unto salvation to every one that believeth"

(Romans 1:16). There is power in the gospel. There is power to stop the sinner in his tracks. There is power to turn a man from the way of death to the way of life, as it is found in the Lord Jesus Christ. There is power to cut and divide. If the gospel can do all of that, we had better know what the gospel is.

A pastor friend in West Virginia told me that the YMCA in his town sets aside a couple of hours each Wednesday for the preachers to play basketball. One day a discussion arose about an accident in which a certain "liberal" preacher had been killed. One of the "liberal" preachers present turned to my friend and asked, "Isn't it awful that such a great preacher of the gospel has been killed?" My friend thought a moment. The dead preacher had been a notorious "liberal." He had been a reprobate in his personal life and an apostate in his theology. Finally my friend said, "The man of whom you speak did not preach the gospel. He did not even know the gospel." A heated argument ensued, and my friend said, "You say that your friend preached the gospel. Let me ask you a question: What is the gospel?" The unbelieving preacher began to stammer. "Well, uh, uh ... it's over there in the Book of The Revelation somewhere. I just can't put my finger on it right now." With that kind of ignorance in the pulpit, no wonder we have people in the pews who are spiritually confused and living in the darkness of their sins!

If the gospel is true, all that contradicts it is false. You cannot merge the thesis of the gospel with its antithesis and form a synthesis, though many people are trying to do that. They are seeking a common ground between the gospel and that which contradicts the gospel. To reconcile the true gospel and a social gospel is impossible. The two are incompatible. To try to synthesize the thesis and the antithesis is to have another gospel; yet there is not another gospel (Galatians 1:7). There is only one gospel. You have *the* gospel or you have a lie.

Paul gives a concise definition of the gospel in I Corinthians 15:3, 4, "that Christ died for our sins according to the scriptures; And that he was buried, and that he rose again the third day according to the scriptures." Lucius Annaeus Seneca, the great Roman philosopher and writer of tragedies, said, "All my life I have been seeking to climb out of the pit of my besetting sins, and I can't do it; and I never will unless a hand is let down to draw me up." The gospel is the good news that God, with His own hand, has let His Son down to this earth to draw men unto Himself. Yet there are multitudes who will not believe the gospel. If the gospel is to save you, you must believe it. Scripture says to "believe on the Lord Jesus Christ, and thou shalt be saved" (Acts 16:31).

I heard of a "liberal" preacher in Brooklyn, New York, who met a poor dying woman. For many years this woman had provided for her family by washing clothes. Long hours of scrubbing clothes at the washboard had scarred her hands. On her deathbed she was asking this "liberal" preacher if Jesus Christ would accept her. "Of course He will accept you," the preacher answered. "You show Him your poor hands, and

He will let you into heaven." That was the worst
advice the woman could have received; yet it is
the only comfort a "liberal" preacher can give.
Imagine this poor woman at the judgment,
having nothing to show the Lord but her tired,
worn, and scarred hands. That is not enough, my
dear friends. The hands of the blessed Lord were
scarred for you. In His hands are the nailprints
from Calvary's cross where He poured out His
life's blood for you. His blood has power to
cleanse from all sin (I John 1:7). That is the
gospel.

Many people try to serve the Lord apart from
the gospel. They seek to enter heaven another
way. In Matthew 7:21-23 the Lord Jesus says,
"Not every one that saith unto me, Lord, Lord,
shall enter into the kingdom of heaven; but he
that doeth the will of my Father which is in
heaven. Many will say to me in that day, Lord,
Lord, have we not prophesied in thy name? and
in thy name have cast out devils? and in thy
name done many wonderful works? And then
will I profess unto them, I never knew you: de-
part from me, ye that work iniquity." It is not on
the basis of wonderful works, tired and scarred
hands from doing good deeds, or sincerity of
heart that God will judge men. He will judge
them on the basis of the gospel. Romans 2:16
warns of a day "when God shall judge the secrets
of men by Jesus Christ according to my gospel."

In the summer of 1939 an American sub-
marine was undergoing some tests off the coast
of New Hampshire. A veteran crew had maneu-
vered her through eighteen successful dives, and
a final emergency test dive was to be made. The

green lights of the control panel indicated "Go!" But when the ship made the dive, two large apertures failed to close, causing the engine room to fill with water. The guard at the bulkhead did what he was supposed to do, and that was to close a great iron door to hold the water in the engine room. Twenty-seven men died in that compartment to save the thirty-three men who remained on board. A diving bell descended 240 feet to pull the remaining men to safety. None of the men who were rescued asked about the maintenance or mechanics of the bell; they wanted to know if it could save them. IT DID!

The gospel is not to be examined or questioned; it is to be believed. I plead with you to believe it.

Question 6

What is a Fundamentalist?

Throughout this book you will find the term "Fundamentalist." For a man to say that he is a Fundamentalist (that is, a Bible-believing Christian) is one thing; for him to perform like a Fundamentalist is an entirely different thing. Unless a man takes the position of Fundamentalism, his profession is meaningless.

I want to discuss with you the position that a Fundamentalist must take in the light of contemporary society. If a man is a Bible-believing Christian who honors the Word of God and uses the Word as it should be used—as the touchstone of truth by which he compares all things—his theological imperative will be a militant orthodoxy. Also, that man will be set on fire with soulwinning zeal. My grandfather used to say, "It takes evangelistic unction to make orthodoxy function." The worst thing in the world is dead orthodoxy—orthodoxy that claims to believe the cardinal truths of the Bible but lacks the evangelistic zeal that is necessary to take this truth to a lost and dying world.

A man who is a fair-minded Fundamentalist will allow for differences of Scriptural *interpretation* in areas that may be subject to interpretation. But there are certain basic doctrines that are not subject to interpretation. Among these are the virgin birth, the essential deity of Christ, the blood atonement, the bodily resurrection from the grave, and the verbal inspiration of Scripture. These are not optional. They are cardinal doctrines that are essential to the new birth. But there are some other things that are matters of interpretation. For example, the Baptists have one interpretation of church polity and the Presbyterians have another. A Fundamentalist will not quibble about such matters of interpretation as long as they are not doctrines that are essential to obtaining salvation.

A Fundamentalist also will hold to and defend truth while being concerned for the salvation of lost men and women. In the process, he will oppose all that is contrary to truth. He will oppose any form of government which would make man dependent upon the state rather than upon God. The Psalmist says, "The Lord is my shepherd; I shall not want. He maketh me to lie down in green pastures ... He restoreth my soul." Note that it is the Lord Who keeps us and provides for our needs. It is not the state that does it. So a Fundamentalist will cherish religious liberty and the right of self-determination.

Next, a Fundamentalist will oppose all sin and vice that would degrade and destroy man. Our society is beset with many social ills. We have the evils of liquor, drugs, and rock music. The sinful rock music with which we are plagued is designed to do to man's emotions—his ability to control himself—what dope and liquor do. What a sad commentary it is on a day that would allow men to set to rock music some quasi-religious words and bring the result into the church on the basis that "this will appeal to men." The only appeal it will have is the appeal that hard rock music has to men's flesh. You do not appeal to the spirit of man by having rock music in the church, you appeal to his flesh. The practice of "gospel" words being set to rock music is the practice of the ecumenical and social gospel. It has no place in the music of the fundamental gospel, the Word of God.

Then, the Fundamentalist will oppose all governmental usurpation over our children. The Fundamentalist vehemently maintains that parenthood is sacred and that God has set children in subjection to the will of their parents. I am deeply concerned by the encroachments of our government in passing laws—on both the federal and the state levels—that would shift control and care of our children from the parents to the state. God says that "children are an heritage of the Lord" and that the control and discipline of those children is the responsibility of the parents, not the prerogative of the state.

Again, a Fundamentalist will oppose the current twisting of the role of women. He will oppose the ERA, the Women's Lib Movement, and the ordination of women into the ministry of the gospel. All of these things are forbidden by Scripture. According to I Timothy 3:2, a bishop (or preacher) is to be "the husband of one wife"; and this would be difficult for a woman preacher.

Our choicest right, guaranteed by the Bill of Rights, is the freedom of religion. The Fundamentalist will oppose anything that would deprive us of that right. He will condemn the turning into a holiday the Lord's Day, which is a holy day. He will condemn any government—the Russian government, the Chinese government, the Eastern European governments, or any other government—that would deny to people the right to worship on the first day of the week and rest from their secular labor.

The Fundamentalist will also oppose the devilish origin and deception of paraphrases and perversions of the Holy Scriptures. I refer to *Good News for Modern Man, The Living Bible, The Revised Standard Version of the Bible,* and *The New English Bible;* these are not accurate translations of the Hebrew and Greek, but perversions that would water down the gospel and rob God's Holy Word of its fundamental truths.

A Fundamentalist will oppose unbiblical ecumenical evangelism and the blasphemies, idolatries, and superstitions of all false religions, among which are the cults and mystical meditations that prevail in our day.

Finally, the Fundamentalist will oppose the cheap, worldly approach to living that falsely calls itself Christian. Yes, a Bible-believing Christian will take positions that are unpopular and that often will put him at cross-purposes with society and with some churches, because those churches have tipped their hats to the world in the interest of not offending people in the pew by telling them what they need to hear. Ecumenical religion—the religion of Antichrist— tells man what he *wants* to hear—that he is basically good and that he can pull himself up by his own bootstraps. God declares that "all have sinned, and come short of the glory of God" (Romans 3:23) and that "there is none righteous, no, not one" (Romans 3:10). Scripture condemns all mankind as guilty before God. The good news of Scripture is that Christ bore our sins "in his own body on the tree [Cross], that we, being dead to sins, should live unto righteousness" (I Peter 2:24). It is the blood of Jesus Christ, God's Son, that cleanses from all sin (I John 1:7).

Question 7

What is the chief end of man?

Consider this question: "What is the chief end of man?" Scripture gives the answer in Psalm 115:1, "Not unto us, O Lord, not unto us, but unto thy name give glory."

I grow disheartened and disgusted to hear so much preaching on radio and television and in pulpits that seems to be geared to the selfish purposes of the preachers. I am a preacher, and many of my best friends are preachers. But there are some preachers who would have to be categorized as "con" artists. They emphasize happiness, joy, success, wealth, and health; but they never discuss the Scriptural obligations of Christian living. God has put us in this world to bring glory to His Name. He does not want any man to seek personal glory.

It is the purpose of the preacher to point

people to Jesus Christ. John the Baptist pointed to our Lord and said, "Behold the Lamb of God, which taketh away the sin of the world" (John 1:29b). But it is not only the *preacher's* job to point men to Jesus Christ and bring glory to His Name; it is also the responsibility of the *Christian layman* to point men to the Son of God and honor Him in daily living. Does your home bring glory to Jesus Christ? Can you, as a Christian, continue in your present job and bring glory to His Name, or are you earning your livelihood in a profession that turns people away from the Lord and a clean, decent life? What kind of contribution are you making with your life to the glory of God? If you are not winning people to Jesus Christ, you are not bringing glory to His Name.

The Psalmist says in Psalm 79:9, "Help us, O God of our salvation, for the glory of thy name: and deliver us, and purge away our sins, for thy name's sake." I shall never forget the first time that the Holy Spirit spoke to me through this verse. Today most soulwinning efforts emphasize only that the person won to Christ will be helped. He *will* be helped. A multitude of sins will be covered with the blood of Jesus Christ. A sinner will be turned from hell into eternal life with Jesus Christ. But that is not the only reason for winning people to Christ: we ought to win souls for *His Name's sake*. With every soul that is snatched from the brink of hell and brought into a personal relationship with Jesus Christ, glory is brought to our Lord.

In order to bring glory to our Lord through soulwinning effort, we must win souls *according to the Word of God.* Ecumenical soulwinning efforts that unite believers and unbelievers in sponsorship and that preach only a vague "religious" message are not an honor to Jesus Christ. Scripture asks, "What communion hath light with darkness? And what concord hath Christ with Belial [Satan]? . . . Wherefore come out from among them, and be ye separate, saith the Lord . . . and I will receive you" (II Corinthians 6:14-17). I cannot bring glory to Christ through a soulwinning effort that brings together light and darkness, Christ and the devil, and that obliterates scriptural lines of separation. Yet that is the practice of almost every modern mass evangelistic crusade. Christians should not support such efforts. We should not give our money, our prayers, or our time to the success of any crusade that is contrary to the Word of God in its message or method. To bring glory to Jesus Christ, we must do His work His way.

To what church do you belong? If your church denies Jesus Christ, mocks His Word or lines up with a denominational program that is sponsoring schools that are sending people to hell and training people for the devil's work, you do not bring glory to Christ by attending that church. You should not support a denominational program that is exalted above the person of the Lord Jesus Christ and that urges cooperation, no matter what that denomination does. Never cooperate with any religious effort that is contrary to the Word of God.

Are you bringing glory to Jesus Christ? If you are disobeying God's Word, you are not glorifying Him. The end does not justify the means. In order to bring glory to Jesus Christ, you must do God's work God's way. I pray that you will get your life and your practice in line with the Bible so that you will glorify the Lord Jesus Christ; for that is the purpose of your presence in this world.

Question 8

Is there a difference between serving God with all your heart and serving Him IN TRUTH with all your heart?

The answer to our question is that there *is* a difference; it determines whether you get heavenly reward for your earthly labor. However, the difference is not recognized by many people who are serving Christ today. The problem is not that they are serving Him insincerely, or that they do not mean well, but that they are serving Him apart from the commands of the Word of God.

If I had to describe present-day Christianity, I would have to call it "gut" Christianity—Christianity which people practice and to which they respond out of a sense of instinct, a sense of feeling. Seeing a need, they do their best to meet the need; but they fail to consult the Word of God in order to see how *He* expects the work to be done.

Failure to follow God's prescribed plan was the downfall of Saul, King of Israel. When Saul was anointed Israel's king, the prophet Samuel, God's spokesman, assembled all the people of Israel, saying to them, "Only fear the Lord, and serve him in truth with all your heart: for consider how great things he hath done for you" (I Samuel 12:24). It is not enough merely to serve the Lord with all your heart; you must serve Him *in truth* with all your heart.

Two years after Samuel had spoken these words, King Saul found himself in a desperate situation. His son Jonathan had attacked a garrison of the Philistines; and the Philistine army had become angry and assembled 30,000 chariots, 6,000 horsemen, and a host of men to go against Israel. Israel's small army became frightened, and they retreated. Saul called His people together to await the prophet Samuel, who had said, "I will be there in seven days." According to Scripture,

> And he [Saul] tarried seven days, according to the set time that Samuel had appointed: but Samuel came not to Gilgal; and the people were scattered from him. And Saul said, Bring hither a burnt-offering to me, and peace-offerings. And he offered the burnt-offering. And it came to pass, that as soon as he had made an end of offering the burnt-offering, behold, Samuel came; and Saul went out to meet him, that he might salute him [or greet him]. And Samuel said, What hast thou done? And Saul said, Because I saw

that the people were scattered from me,
and that thou camest not within the
days appointed, and that the Philistines
gathered themselves together at
Michmash; Therefore said I, The Philistines will come down now upon me to
Gilgal, and I have not made supplica-
tion unto the Lord: I forced myself
therefore, and offered a burnt-offering.
And Samuel said to Saul, Thou hast
done foolishly: thou hast not kept the
commandment of the Lord thy God,
which he commanded thee: for now
would the Lord have established thy
kingdom upon Israel for ever. But now
thy kingdom shall not continue: the
Lord hath sought him a man after his
own heart, and the Lord hath commanded him to be captain over his
people, because thou hast not kept that
which the Lord commanded thee
(I Samuel 13:8-14).

What wrong act had Saul performed? He had
intruded into the priest's office. Having been
king for two years, Saul apparently had devel-
oped a feeling of infallibility about himself.
Rulers, presidents, and governing bodies often
get the feeling that they cannot do wrong. They
begin to feel omniscient and all powerful. Saul
was Israel's king, not a prophet or priest; yet he
took to himself the prophet's office. When Samuel
rebuked him, Saul returned the rebuke, saying,
"If you had come on time, Samuel, I would not
have had to do this thing." Because he disobeyed
God, Saul lost his kingdom; but instead of blam-

ing himself, he blamed God's prophet. Hosts of people who sin will not admit to sin within themselves. They look at the sins of others and blame them. Some of you are guilty of that sin. Instead of turning the conviction to yourselves, you turn it away. That is the wrong way to handle conviction.

Saul was a guilty man, and Samuel said, "God is going to punish you, Saul." "What have I done?" Saul asked. "The people were scattered, and you tarried your coming. It seemed reasonable that if our lives were in danger, we should offer a sacrifice to God." Offering the sacrifice was a good thing in itself, but it was the prophet's job. For the king to do that which God had assigned to the prophets was blasphemy. It was an insult to God.

God is very jealous that His work be done in His way. If Saul had waited only an hour or two longer, he would not have lost his kingdom. But he wanted to do something for God. He reasoned that there was a need. The need was legitimate, but he did not meet it God's way, and God was displeased. Some of you may think that God was unjust to Saul, that Saul's act was not worthy of such severe punishment. In God's sight there is no little sin, for there is no little God to sin against.

I am speaking to some sincere Christians who see a world that is dying and on its way to hell. You say, "These people need to be won to Christ." You are right. It is the task of this generation to get to a lost and dying world the good news that Jesus Christ died on Calvary's Cross and shed His blood in order that we might have the remission of sin. But that task must be done in obedience to God's Word. To do the work of God in a way that is contrary to His Word is to face punishment for your good intentions. God will not reward you for work that you have done in *your* way instead of God's way.

God's judgment on Saul demonstrates that it is not enough to serve the Lord sincerely out of your heart; you must serve Him *in truth* with all your heart. God's Word is truth. If you seek to serve the Lord contrary to the Bible, you are not serving Him in truth. Oh, you may be serving Him sincerely. You may be staying in a "liberal" church with the intention of reaching some people for Jesus Christ. You do not believe what the man in the pulpit is teaching, but you feel that you can counteract it by telling people what is right. The Lord did not tell you to stay in that "liberal" church that denies His Son. He said to "come out from among them, and be ye separate, saith the Lord, and touch not the unclean thing; and I will receive you" (II Corinthians 6:7). You should get out of your "liberal" churches and join a good Bible-believing church. Stop serving the Lord out of a "gut feeling" for what needs to be done. You have the reliable Word of God. Serve the Lord *in truth* with all your heart.

Question 9

Should Christians judge others?

There is much misunderstanding with regard to judging, and I want to use God's Word to clarify the issue. Perhaps our question would be better stated in the words, "Dare a Christian not judge?"

In John 14:15 our Lord says, "If ye love me, keep my commandments." Our love for the Lord can be measured only by our obedience to His Word. Luke 18:1 commands us to pray. Acts 1:8 commands us to witness. Hebrews 10:25 commands us to assemble ourselves together in fellowship around His Word. It is important to understand that all Christians who seek God's favor must obey the commands of Scripture.

To answer the question, "Should Christians judge others?" let us consider John 7:24, "Judge not according to the appearance, but judge righ-

teous judgment." According to this verse, we do
not have the option of judging or not judging; we
are to judge. The command is positive, "Judge
righteous judgment." In other words, we are not
to look at a person or movement that claims to be
of Christ and say, "According to *my* way of
thinking," or, "By *my* opinion that is good or
bad." My grandfather, who founded Bob Jones
University, used to say, "Never judge things by
what you see; judge what you see by what God's
Word says about what you see." There is a wrong
way and a right way to judge.

If we judge things in the light of Scripture, we
will judge righteous judgment. Some people
argue that "in Matthew 7:1 the Lord says to
'judge not, that ye be not judged.'" We do not
have the right to isolate a verse from its context
in order to prove a point. The context says,

> Judge not, that ye be not judged. For
> with what judgment ye judge, ye shall
> be judged: and with what measure ye
> mete, it shall be measured to you again.
> And why beholdest thou the mote that
> is in thy brother's eye, but considerest
> not the beam that is in thine own eye?
> Or how wilt thou say to thy brother,
> Let me pull out the mote out of thine
> eye; and, behold, a beam is in thine
> own eye? Thou hypocrite, first cast out
> the beam out of thine own eye; and
> then shalt thou see clearly to cast out
> the mote out of thy brother's eye. Give
> not that which is holy unto the dogs,
> neither cast ye your pearls before
> swine, lest they trample them under

their feet, and turn again and rend
you" (vv. 1-6).

To "judge not, that ye be not judged" simply
means that you must not judge hypocritically.
That is, you must be sure that your own life is in
line with God's Word before you try to help
somebody else get his life in line with God's
Word. First you must cast the *log* from your own
eye so that you will be able to see clearly to cast
the *splinter* from your brother's eye.

If "judge not, that ye be not judged" referred
to not making discernments, why would the Lord
add, "Give not that which is holy unto dogs,
neither cast ye your pearls before swine"
(v. 6)? In order to obey the latter command, a
distinction—judgment—must be made. You must
judge what it is you cast your pearls and holy
things to.

In the Greek language the word for *judge* in
Matthew 7:1 has a legal connotation. It means
"to try, to condemn, to sentence." According to
Scripture, you and I do not have the right to sentence a man—to consign him to hell. The Lord is
the righteous judge; and in the final judgment He
will hand down the proper sentence. In this
world, however, we are to make discernments
and be spiritually discriminating.

Paul wrote to the Corinthians, "But he that is
spiritual judgeth all things, yet he himself is
judged of no man. For who hath known the mind
of the Lord, that he may instruct him? But we
have the mind of Christ" (I Corinthians 2:15, 16).
The Greek word for *judge* in this passage means
"to interrogate, to scrutinize, to investigate." It is
a mark of spirituality to examine all things

through the microscope of God's Word and say, "According to the Bible, this is right and that is wrong." An obedient Christian has both the right and the obligation to make that kind of judgment. A carnal or gullible Christian, however, makes his judgments on the basis of outward appearances.

What qualifies you to make spiritual judgment? Paul answers, "We have the mind of the Lord." God's Word is the mind of the Lord; and when you make a judgment according to God's Word, you judge not on the basis of the way things look, but on the basis of God's description of the way those things look in His eyes. Romans 2:2 says, "But we are sure that the judgment of God is according to truth." If your judgments are made on the basis of the Word of God, you can be sure that those judgments are according to truth.

As the child of God, you must obey His Word and judge righteous judgments. That is the only way to stay out of spiritual trouble and have the Lord's blessing on your life. Making your judgments according to the Word of God will keep you from running with the wrong crowd, joining the wrong kind of church, and sending money to support the wrong kind of Christian endeavor. God help you to judge righteous judgment.

Question 10

Should preachers name names from the pulpit?

My grandfather used to say, "There is nothing wrong in America that straight preaching could not cure." The trouble is that it is hard to find a straight preacher anymore. Too many preachers are greasing the wheels of the denomination and tickling the fancy of the hearers in the pews. Instead of telling people "Thus saith the Lord," they are telling people what they think the people want to hear.

The responsibility of the preacher is not *originality,* but *fidelity* to the Word of God which is forever settled in heaven (Psalm 119:89). When men are straight preachers, they will name sin and also name sinners. If they do not name sin and sinners, they are not faithful proclaimers of God's Word.

Paul says in I Corinthians 1:21, "It pleased

God by the foolishness of preaching to save them
that believe." The right kind of preaching will
always seem foolish to people who have stiff
necks that refuse to bend, deaf ears that do not
want to hear the truth, and hearts that do not
want to believe it. There are always preachers
who are tools of the devil. These preachers are
vultures to snatch away the seed of the gospel
before it takes root. Men like that abound in the
religious hierarchy of just about every major
denomination in America. Faithful preachers of
the gospel should name religious deceivers and
expose them.

The Apostle Paul says in Romans 16:17,
"Mark them which cause divisions and offences
contrary to the doctrine which ye have learned;
and avoid them. For they that are such serve not
our Lord Jesus Christ." A faithful preacher of the
Word will name men of unsound doctrine and
unscriptural practice. He will expose these men
so that his people who really love the Lord can
avoid them.

The New Testament cites at least three kinds
of people who were named in the preaching of
the apostles in the early church. They named
men who deserted God's work for the world. In
II Timothy 4:10 Paul declares, "Demas hath for-
saken me, having loved this present world, and
is departed unto Thessalonica." They named *men
who hindered God's work by direct opposition.*
Paul said in II Timothy 4:14, "Alexander the
coppersmith did me much evil: the Lord reward
him according to his works." And they named
men who used God's work for personal gain.
III John 9, "But Diotrephes, who loveth to have

the preeminence among them, receiveth us not."
Diotrephes would not permit Paul to preach in
his pulpit. Why? Diotrephes was a jealous man.
He was afraid that somebody might think that
Paul was a better preacher than he was. For the
sake of personal gain, therefore, Diotrephes was
hostile toward those who were also of the house-
hold of faith. Demas, Alexander the coppersmith,
and Diotrephes were named as enemies of the
gospel, and faithful preachers today will not fail
to rebuke sinners by name.

The world criticizes pastors who name names
in the pulpit; yet the world does not hesitate to
name names when it is to their own profit.
Recently the Literary Guild, a national book club
of a million and a quarter members, introduced
a new book entitled *Past Forgetting*. This book
supposedly contains "the true story of Kay
Summersby Morgan and her war-time love affair
with past President Dwight Eisenhower." Says
Kay Morgan, "I was always extremely discreet;
but now that the General is dead and I am dying,
I would like the world to know the truth." How
dark and evil the hour when people write books
to brag about their sin! I do not care how erudite
and advanced people of the 20th century think
they are; in God's sight sin is as evil as it has
always been, and it will be punished.

Paul said to Timothy, "Them that sin rebuke
before all, that others also may fear" (I Timothy
5:20). Preachers must never be intimidated from
preaching the scriptural way, and that includes
naming names from the pulpit so that the
hearers may avoid them. If you do not have such
a man of God for your preacher, find one.

Question 11

Who is the god of the ecumenical church?

Ecumenicity is the religious fad of our day. In the minds of most people, ecumenicity is good. In the mind of God, it is bad. Every attempt that man has ever made to unite the world religiously has been cursed of God.

Let us briefly consider what the Bible teaches about man's efforts to bring his world together. Back in the days of the tower of Babel (Genesis 11) man sought to build a city and a tower to god. But man wanted to be the god of the structure and of the city and people he was seeking to bring together. This tower was an insult to God, and God destroyed and dispersed the people and confused their language.

A world that is united under man's hand will always be a world that leaves God out. Nebuchadnezzar, of whom we read in Daniel 4, ordered the building of a large image of gold. According to historians, this image was made in the likeness of Nebuchadnezzar and was 85 feet high. Nebuchadnezzar issued orders that at an appointed time all of his kingdom should send representatives to a great festival to be held on the plain of Dura in honor of this new image. This was intended by Nebuchadnezzar as a uniting of the kingdom in one religion. When the musical instruments began to sound, all the people were to bow down and worship this image. Thank God, three men refused to bow. Shadrach, Meshach, and Abednego chose to face death rather than bow down to an ecumenical god.

Scripture speaks of a day when antichrist, the "man of sin," will come to the end of his seven-year rule during which he will have held sway over the Western empire of the world and will be destroyed and cast into hell. Scripture calls this antichrist "the beast." Revelation 19:20 says, "And the beast was taken, and with him the false prophet that wrought miracles before him, with which he deceived them that had received the mark of the beast, and them that worshipped his image. These both were cast alive into a lake of fire burning with brimstone." A day will come when antichrist will make his final attempt to bring the world together under a federated political head, which will also have its religious head. There is also a false prophet who rules alongside the beast. This false prophet is the religious head of the ecumenical world. But eventually both the false prophet and the beast (or antichrist) will be cast together into an eternal hell which God has prepared for the devil and his angels. Those who build ecumenical churches do the devil's work; and if your god is not the devil, you should not be in those ecumenical churches worshipping at the devil's altar.

If there were many ways to God, ecumenicity would be all right. But there is only one way to God. That way is Jesus Christ (John 14:6). If there were many ways to God, we could afford to join hands with all religions. Each could go to God his own way while holding hands with others who were trying to get to God their own way. But there is only one way. Thus, if salvation is by Jesus Christ's shed blood alone, all who are seeking to go to heaven another way will be sadly and eternally disappointed. They will go instead to their ruin and damnation.

Jesus Christ said, "I am the way, the truth, and the life: no man cometh unto the Father, but by me" (John 14:6). Jesus Christ is the Lord of the true church. Without Him there is no true church. Paul says, "For other foundation can no man lay than that is laid, which is Jesus Christ" (I Corinthians 3:11).

I say this reverently, but with the full authority of Scripture: God is a separatist. In Acts 17:26, 27 the Apostle Paul, preaching to the Athenians, says that God "hath made of one blood all nations of men for to dwell on all the face of the earth, and hath determined the times before appointed, and the bounds of their habitation; That they should seek the Lord, if haply they might feel after him." God's purpose in dividing people is that they might seek after Him. When in their ecumenical madness men get together, they unite apart from the authority of

the deity of Jesus Christ and His shed blood.
Men in an ecumenical church may seek after
their denominational machinery. They may seek
after some kind of religious assurances. They
may revel in the false hope of good works and
think that all is well with God. But the god of the
ecumenical church is Satan; and the ecumenical
church is being built to overthrow the true
church, the church of Jesus Christ.

Revelation 13:3, 4 says that "all the world
wondered after the beast. And they worshipped
the dragon which gave power unto the beast: and
they worshipped the beast, saying, Who is like
unto the beast?" The dragon, or the serpent, is
Satan. Satan, in the form of a serpent, intruded
into the world in the garden of Eden, beguiling
and deceiving Adam and Eve. Throughout Scripture we see Satan deceiving and destroying men.
God warns of a day when those who have sought
after Satan's deception and have belonged to and
promoted ecumenical churches will be cast into
hell along with the dragon who empowers antichrist who in the end times—the time in which
we live—seeks to build the ecumenical church.

The spirit of antichrist is at work today building the ecumenical church; and he, antichrist,
and Satan who has deceived the nations, will be
cast into hell.

The beast is antichrist. The ecumenical church
is the church of antichrist, bringing all men together regardless of their religious beliefs and
doctrinal differences. Jesus Christ is the dividing
line between those who are saved and those who
are lost. The church without Christ is the church
of antichrist, and the spirit of ancient Babel is

the spirit of the ecumenical church. The goals of the present ecumenical church are the same as those of the tower of Babel. And as God destroyed man's effort at Babel, so will He destroy the effort of the ecumenical church.

Bob Jones University obviously is opposed to the ecumenical church. If you are opposed to it, you ought to get out of it. I hope that you are not in it; but if you are in, get out. The Bible says to "come out from among them, and be ye separate, saith the Lord, and touch not the unclean thing; and I will receive you" (II Corinthians 6:17). If you are a part of a National Council of Churches congregation or one of those churches that cooperates with ecumenicity, get out of it. If *Christ* is not there, and you belong to Him, *you* ought not to be there.

If you are a young person who wants to serve Jesus Christ and be found faithful in His service, you must be separated from the ecumenical church. You need to be in a school like Bob Jones University to get your training. At Bob Jones University they will train you in how to win souls and how to take biblical and Christ-honoring stands so that your life and ministry can stand approved in the sight of God.

Question 12

Should Christians worry about who antichrist is?

Let me preface our Scripture reading by saying that Christians do not need to worry about the identity of antichrist. Scripture does not reveal his name, but it says much about world conditions prior to and during antichrist's coming as well as about the character of his seven-year reign. A typical passage is II Thessalonians 2:2-12:

> The day of Christ is at hand. Let no man deceive you by any means: for that day shall not come, except there come a falling away first, and that man of sin be revealed, the son of perdition; Who opposeth and exalteth himself above all that is called God, or that is worshipped; so that he as God sitteth in the temple of God, shewing

himself that he is God. Remember ye
not, that, when I was yet with you,
I told you these things? And now ye
know what withholdeth that he might
be revealed in his time. For the mystery
of iniquity doth already work: only he
who now letteth [hindereth] will
let [hinder], until he be taken out of the
way. And then shall that Wicked [one]
be revealed, whom the Lord shall con-
sume with the spirit of his mouth, and
shall destroy with the brightness of his
coming: Even him, whose coming
is after the working of Satan with
all power and signs and lying wonders,
And with all deceivableness of unrighteousness in them that perish; because
they received not the love of the truth,
that they might be saved. And for this
cause God shall send them strong
delusion, that they should believe a lie:
That they all might be damned who believed not the truth, but had pleasure in
unrighteousness.

Let us consider the *conditions* of antichrist's
coming. Verse 3 describes the religious condition
that makes possible his coming and accompanies
his coming: "Let no man deceive you by any
means: for that day [the day of the earthly rule of
Jesus Christ] shall not come, except there come a
falling away first, and that man of sin, the son of
perdition, be revealed." The term "falling away"
suggests an apostate condition that comes over
the world religiously. Today the Christian church
is largely apostate. Oh, God has His remnant—

the fundamental, Bible-believing Christian church—but most of the denominations of the day have become apostate. These denominations have fallen away from the doctrine and truth of God's Word and have substituted the thinking of man. This falling away (apostasy) must reach full bloom before the man of sin, or antichrist, can be revealed.

Another religious occurrence before that time can come is that the Holy Spirit must be taken out of the world. Verse 6, "And now ye know what withholdeth that he might be revealed in his time." If the coming of Christ is on the threshold—and I believe that it is—antichrist is already in the world, and it is only a matter of time until he is revealed. But something is standing in the way of his being revealed. Verse 7 explains, "For the mystery of iniquity doth already work: only he who now [hindereth] will [hinder], until he be taken out of the way." The hinderer is the Holy Spirit of God. I Corinthians 6:19 asks, "What? know ye not that your body is the temple of the Holy Ghost?" The Holy Spirit lives in all genuinely born-again believers. Until the Holy Spirit is taken out of the world, antichrist cannot come in his force. Oh, the mystery of iniquity is at work (v. 7); sinfulness is spreading throughout the earth at unprecedented pace, and the world is getting ready for antichrist. But antichrist cannot be revealed until first the Holy Spirit is taken out of the way. This involves the rapture of the Church, when Christians, in whom the Holy Spirit resides, are taken out of the world. Antichrist will come then in full force to do his worst in the world.

Next, let us consider the *character* of his coming. Verse 4 says that he "opposeth and exaltest himself above all that is called God, or that is worshipped: so that he as God sitteth in the temple of God, shewing himself that he is God." Antichrist's reign will be characterized by *blasphemy*. Religious blasphemy abounds in our modern world. The average person of the world takes the Name of Christ in vain and seemingly has no concern about it. He curses God with almost every breath.

Antichrist's rule is also characterized by *brevity*. The Jewish temple will be reconstructed in Jerusalem, and that is the place where antichrist will rule, passing himself off as Christ, as God. According to verse 8, the Lord, when He returns, will destroy that "wicked [one]" with the spirit of His mouth and the brightness of His coming. That is, at the end of antichrist's seven-year rule, the Lord Jesus will return with His saints from heaven, and the darkness of antichrist's rule will be contrasted to the brightness of Christ.

Verses 9 and 10 say that antichrist's rule will be a *deceiving* rule, "Even him, whose coming is after the working of Satan [the underlying power of antichrist is Satan] with all power and signs and lying wonders, And with all deceivableness or unrighteousness in them that perish; because they received not the love of the truth, that they might be saved." Antichrist will deceive people.

Verses 11 and 12 describe his rule as a *damning* rule. "And for this cause God shall send them [people who do not love truth] strong delusion, that they should believe a lie. That they all might be damned who believed not the truth, but had pleasure in unrighteousness." Those who follow Satan will be damned.

Many of you listen to deceptive voices of the religious world, and many of these voices are prominently displayed on television week after week. Some of you attend liberal churches where the voice of antichrist, the voice of Satan, speaks to you. I plead with you to listen to the truth of the Word of God and to receive the Lord Jesus in your heart and be saved.

Question 13

How will the world end?

If you have pondered the question "How will the world end?" you are not the first person to do so. Even the disciples, after they had heard the Lord talk about the destruction of Jerusalem in the end time, became curious about when these things should be. Matthew 24:3 says, "And as he sat upon the mount of Olives, the disciples came unto him privately, saying, Tell us, when shall these things be? and what shall be the sign of thy coming, and of the end of the world?" People have always been curious about the ultimate outcome of man's existence on this planet.

The Bible clearly answers this question. The world will not get better, as some men believe. It will get increasingly worse until ultimately it results in Armageddon. Those who think that this world is going to evolve into a paradise do not know or understand what the Bible teaches on the subject.

The earth began as a paradise. God created it without sin. When Adam and Eve sinned, they placed the planet under the curse and judgment of the holy God of heaven; sin intruded into the original paradise, and the world has been going downward ever since. All of this will be terminated not by a restorer who will come on the scene from among men, but by the Prince of Peace, the Lord Jesus Christ, Who, after the darkness of a period to be known as the Great Tribulation, will appear in the brightness of His glory.

I would like to rehearse for you the chain of events which the Bible says will transpire. The Bible makes it clear that prior to the tribulation, the Church (that is, all born-again believers) will be raptured from the world. This rapture could take place at any moment. Yes, the personal coming of Jesus Christ in the heavens for His redeemed, ransomed bride—the born-again Church—is imminent.

Following this rapture there will be on earth a period of seven years which will be divided into two parts. The first three-and-a-half-year period will consist of a time of relative peace in the world. The Western European nations will be gathered together under the rule of a personality to be known as "the man of sin," "the son of perdition," "the antichrist." This personality will appear to give an answer to man's most severe problems, to bring relative peace to the world. He will sign a treaty of peace with the nation Israel. During that time Israel will feel satisfied that she is finally safe from any kind of war, and she will dwell in unwalled villages (Ezekiel 38:11, 14). She will trust Arab nations and all other nations as her friends.

Suddenly, in the middle of that period, the antichrist will turn against Israel and will declare war against her. His attempt to come against her will be for the sake of the treasures—the oil and mineral reserves (Ezekiel 38:10-12)—of the Middle East. This attempt, as well as Russia's attempt to come down, will be aborted. Russia will be turned around; Scripture says that God will put a hook in her jaw and turn her back (Ezekiel 38:4).

The troubles of the earth will continue to mount until finally they will culminate in what will be World War III, or, as the Bible calls it, Armageddon. A European confederation under the antichrist will send its armies against Israel. Also, Russia will send her armies against Israel. The Bible says in Revelation 9:16 that some two million soldiers, under the authority of the King of the East, will also march against the Middle East. From the south (that is, Africa) armies will come up; and there in the Middle East, in the plain of Megiddo (a small, tranquil place of some five or six miles across and fifteen miles in length), Armageddon will take place. The armies of the nations will think that they are coming to make war against each other; but I believe the Bible clearly teaches that Satan brings these armies together, knowing that the return of the Lord Jesus with His heavenly hosts is imminent. I believe that the devil brings these armies into the Middle East to do war against the armies of heaven, to literally "shoot them out of the sky" if he could.

Just before the Lord Jesus appears in the heaven, this time not suddenly and invisible to the whole world, as in the rapture, but in the brightness of His glory, there will be severe earthquakes. Cities will literally fall into the sea. The earth will heave and be caught in great judgment; the battle of Armageddon will take place; and the armies of the nations will be slain. So great will be the carnage of that time that in the plain of Megiddo the blood will flow to the horses' bridles (Revelation 13:20). Then the sun will be blotted out; the moon will lose her light; and the earth—in the darkness—will see appearing in the heavens the Lord Jesus at the head of the great procession of the ransomed saints and the angels of glory (Matthew 24:29; Luke 21:25-27). Our Lord will march, for all the world to see, from heaven to earth. According to Daniel 2, He will set His feet upon this earth, will set up His kingdom in Jerusalem, and will rule the nations of the world. At that time He will judge both the unbelieving Jews and the unbelieving Gentiles. But the remnant of Jews who have come to believe on Him during the tribulation and the Gentiles who have received Him and have helped the Jews and sheltered them from persecution during that period will be left; and for a period of one thousand years the earth will be under the rule of the righteousness of the Son of Glory, the Lord Jesus Christ. Our Lord will prove to the world what it could have had if it had not turned its back on Him, refused His authority, and turned to sin—"every man turning unto his own way."

According to II Peter 3:10, "the day of the Lord will come as a thief in the night; in the which the heavens shall pass away with a great noise, and the elements shall melt with fervent heat, the earth also and the works that are therein shall be burned up." At the end of the millennium there will be on the earth a heat so strong that it will turn the earth to a cinder. The earth will be burned in the fire of God's judgment, and there will be "a new heaven and a new earth" for which we, according to His promise, look. The new earth will be an earth wherein dwelleth righteousness.

A holy God must judge sin. This earth is under the judgment and curse of sin. God has spared His judgment for a time, giving man a day of grace wherein he might be able to trust in the Lord Jesus Christ. The Bible says that "when the fulness of the time was come, God sent forth his Son, made of a woman, made under the law, To redeem them that were under the law" (Galatians 4:4, 5). When the fulness of time came—God's time—the Son of Glory came in human flesh. He was born of a virgin, He lived a sinless life among men, and He died on the Cross to purge man's sin. By the shedding of His blood on the Cross He made atonement so that you and I might have peace with God. If you do not accept His *peace,* you are the object of His *wrath* and will be judged as the earth is judged; for all sin must be judged. God loves the sinner, but He hates sin. A holy God must punish sin and must punish this earth which we sinners have corrupted. But one day He will burn all of it up in the fire of His judgment and there will be a new heaven and a new earth.

Look around you at this earth. It is groaning in travail and pain. There are wars and rumors of wars; and according to Matthew 24, the situation is not going to get any better. Earthquakes will increase and there will be severe pestilence, famine, and persecution of Jews—all of which will lead to the end times when the Lord will return and set up His millennial rule upon the earth and bring the peace which no political party or world system or dictator could ever bring. I commend to you the Prince of Peace, the Lord Jesus Christ.